THEMATIC UNIT
FIVE SENSES

Written by Janet Hale

Illustrated by Theresa Wright, Paula Spence, and Keith Vasconcelles

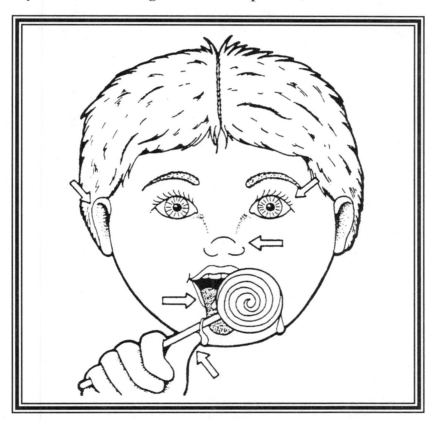

Teacher Created Materials, Inc.
6421 Industry Way
Westminster, CA 92683
www.teachercreated.com

©1990 Teacher Created Materials, Inc.
Reprinted, 2000
Made in U.S.A.

ISBN 1-55734-270-9

Table of Contents

Introduction

Five Senses contains a captivating whole language, thematic unit. Its 80 exciting pages are filled with a wide variety of lesson ideas and activity sheets designed for use with early primary children. At its core are two high-quality children's literature selections, *The Town Mouse and the Country Mouse* and *The Little Red Hen*. For each of these books, activities are included which set the stage for reading, encourage the enjoyment of the book, and extend the concepts gained. In addition, the theme is connected to the curriculum with lessons in language arts, math, science, social studies, art, music, and life skills (cooking, physical education, etc.). Many of these activities encourage cooperative learning. Suggestions and patterns for bulletin boards and unit management tools are additional time savers for the busy teacher. Futhermore, directions for student-created Big Books and a culminating activity, which allow students to synthesize their knowledge in order to produce products that can be shared beyond the classroom, highlight this very complete teacher resource.

This thematic unit includes:

- ☐ **literature selections** — summaries of two children's books with related lessons (complete with reproducible pages) that cross the curriculum

- ☐ **poetry** — suggested selections and lessons enabling students to write and publish their own works

- ☐ **planning guides** — suggestions for sequencing lessons each day of the unit

- ☐ **language experience ideas** — daily suggestions as well as activities across the curriculum, including Big Books

- ☐ **bulletin board ideas** — suggestions and plans for student-created and/or interactive bulletin boards

- ☐ **homework suggestions** — extending the unit to the child's home

- ☐ **curriculum connections** — in language arts, math, science, social studies, art, music, and life skills

- ☐ **group projects** — to foster cooperative learning

- ☐ **a culminating activity** — which requires students to synthesize their learning to produce a product or engage in an activity that can be shared with others

- ☐ **a bibliography** — suggesting additional literature and nonfiction books on the theme

To keep this valuable resource intact so that it can be used year after year, you may wish to punch holes in the pages and store them in a three-ring binder.

Introduction *(cont.)*

Why Whole Language?

A whole language approach involves children in using all modes of communication: reading, writing, listening, observing, illustrating, experiencing, and doing. Communication skills are interconnected and integrated into lessons that emphasize the whole of language rather than isolating its parts. The lessons revolve around selected literature. Reading is not taught as a separate subject from writing and spelling, for example. A child reads, writes (spelling appropriately for his/her level), speaks, listens, etc. in response to a literature experience introduced by the teacher. In this way, language skills grow naturally, stimulated by involvement and interest in the topic at hand.

Why Thematic Planning?

One very useful tool for implementing an integrated whole language program is thematic planning. By choosing a theme with correlating literature selections for a unit of study, a teacher can plan activities throughout the day that lead to a cohesive, in-depth study of the topic. Students will be practicing and applying their skills in meaningful contexts. Consequently, they will tend to learn and retain more. Both teachers and students will be freed from a day that is broken into unrelated segments of isolated drill and practice.

Why Cooperative Learning?

Besides academic skills and content, students need to learn social skills. No longer can this area of development be taken for granted. Students must learn to work cooperatively in groups in order to function well in modern society. Group activities should be a regular part of school life and teachers should consciously include social objectives as well as academic objectives in their planning. For example, a group working together to write a report may need to select a leader. The teacher should make clear to the students and monitor the qualities of good leader-follower group interaction just as he/she would state and monitor the academic goals of the project.

Why Big Books?

An excellent cooperative, whole language activity is the production of Big Books. Groups of students, or the whole class, can apply their language skills, content knowledge, and creativity to produce a Big Book that can become a part of the classroom library to be read and reread. These books make excellent culminating projects for sharing beyond the classroom with parents, librarians, other classes, etc. Big Books can be produced in many ways and this thematic unit book includes directions for at least one method you may choose.

The Town Mouse and the Country Mouse

Suggested Version: retold and illustrated by Lorinda Bryan Cauley

Summary

Town Mouse visits his cousin, Country Mouse, who gives a tour and prepares a tasty supper. Town Mouse thinks country living is boring and requires too much hard work. Country Mouse then visits the town, where he is frightened by the bright lights and loud noises. The food is wonderful, but eating it is not pleasant when servants enter, a child peeks, and dogs bark! Country Mouse decides that he prefers his simple country life.

The outline below is a suggested plan for using the various activities that are presented in this unit. You should adapt these ideas to fit your own classroom situations.

Sample Plan

Day I

- Introduce the unit with the bulletin board activity (page 68)
- Play "Senses Simon" (page 6)
- Use puppets to discuss town and country (page 6)
- Read *The Town Mouse and the Country Mouse* aloud
- Use "The Mice Use Their Senses" activity, page 8. Focus on seeing and hearing
- Use the Seeing and Hearing activities on pages 9-11
- My Sense Poem (pages 41-42)

Day II

- Take town and country walks
- Make town and country chart
- Reread *The Town Mouse and the Country Mouse* looking for places where the mice used smelling and tasting
- Use "Mice Use Their Senses" activity, page 8. Focus on smelling and tasting
- Make barley-corn soup and/or carrot cookies (recipes, page 61)
- Make a class language-experience story about cooking
- Homework: Ask students to bring in hard and soft toys
- Do "Smelling and Tasting" activities (pages 12-13)

Day III

- Show and tell hard and soft toys emphasizing sense of touch
- Reread the story looking for "touching" situations
- Use "The Mice Use Their Senses" activity, page 8. Focus on touching
- Do "Feeling and Feeling" activities (pages 14-16)
- Make "When I Feel, I Feel..." books (page 43)
- Have children draw and tell or write about their favorite part of the story

Day IV

- Do sense experience activities from Across the Curriculum section–pages 48-60 (Will take more than one day)
- Make Accordion Book (page 43)
- Discuss the moral of the town and country mouse fable
- Read several other fables to the class
- Study real mice
- Make mice masks (Extension, page 8)
- Culminating Activity: Sensation Stations (pages 63-67)
- Make "My Favorite Sensation Station" class book (page 44)
- Use masks to perform plays of the story

Overview of Activities

SETTING THE STAGE

1. Set the mood by creating the bulletin board display outlined on pages 68-72. Follow the directions on page 68 to use the bulletin board as a unit introduction.

2. Create a Five Senses Learning Center. See page 73 for how-to's.

3. Create a comfy "Senses Reading Corner" by placing pillows and blankets in a corner of the classroom. Fill a basket with picture and literature books that the students may look at during a planned or free time. (See Bibliography, page 79, for suggestions.)

4. Turn the popular children's game "Simon Says" into "Senses Simon" giving directions like, "Senses Simon says, 'Touch your ears,' or 'Touch what you hear with.'"

5. Use mouse puppets to introduce *The Town Mouse and the Country Mouse*. (Directions and patterns for a mouse paper bag puppet are on pages 17 and 27.) As you tell them where the mice are from, encourage the students to describe what it is like to live in the country and to live in a town. What things can they see, hear, smell, taste, and touch in the two environments?

ENJOYING THE BOOK

1. Read *The Town Mouse and the Country Mouse* to the children for enjoyment.

2. Prepare "The Mice Use Their Senses" activity, page 8. Reread the story and use the appropriate questions as you emphasize specific senses.

3. Emphasize seeing and hearing. Show the class a pair of glasses and ask students what they are used for. Then, show a record or tape player and ask what it is used for. Emphasize that we see with the glasses, and we hear the sounds from the player. Do "See and Hear" activities, pages 9-11.

4. Take a "town walk" and a "country walk" around your school. The town walk could be through the school's hallways and rooms, while the country walk could be to a nearby park or school playground. Upon returning from the walks, make a class chart divided into two sections. Label them "Our Town Walk"/"Our Country Walk." Hand out four small sheets of paper to each student and have them illustrate one thing they saw and one thing they heard in the "town" and in the "country." Have each student come up and glue their illustrations to the correct side of the chart.

Overview of Activities *(cont.)*

5. Now, concentrate on smelling and tasting. Reread the story to find places where the mice smell and taste. Use the appropriate questions from ''The Mice Use Their Senses'' page 8. Do smell and taste activities (pages 12-13).

6. Make barley-corn soup and/or carrot cookies (recipes, page 61). Be sure to smell and taste the ingredients before and after they are combined. If these cooking projects are too ambitious, try popping and eating popcorn. Write a class language experience story about your cooking project.

7. Homework: To highlight the sense of touch, have students bring their favorite soft and hard toys from home. Students share during a Show and Tell session allowing classmates to feel the difference between the items.

8. Reread the story looking for ''touching'' situations.

9. Do the ''Feeling and Feelings'' activities on pages 14-16 to help children distinguish between the two meanings of the word ''feel.''

10. Since the students are now very familiar with the story, have them illustrate and write or dictate a sentence or two about their favorite part of the story. Make a graph to show how many liked the same parts. Display the pictures and graph.

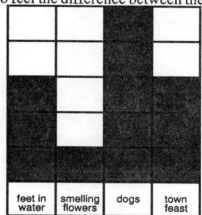

feet in water	smelling flowers	dogs	town feast

EXTENDING THE BOOK

1. Use the sense experiences in the Across the Curriculum section (pages 48-60).

2. ''The Town Mouse and the Country Mouse'' is a famous Aesop Fable. As with all fables, there is a moral to the story. Sharing the moral of this story with younger students may seem difficult. To simplify the idea, explain that, ''it is often better to be thankful for what we have, than to wish for something else.'' Read and discuss other fables.

3. Study real mice. ''Mouse'' comes from the Asian word for ''thief.'' Mice are known for ''stealing'' food and destroying items in people's homes and farmers' fields.

''House mice'' measure 5 to 6 inches in length, including the tail; they weigh between 1/2 and 1 ounce. (Demonstrate these measurements on a ruler, balance, or postal scale.) Their fur is soft, and the tail is covered with scaly skin. Long, thin whiskers grow from the sides of their snouts to help them feel their way through the dark since mice cannot see very well.

It may seem like mice are always eating, but they eat very little. They like the same food as humans.

To make the learning experience more complete, bring in a cage of mice for the students to observe and take care of. Have an oral sharing time about what they see the mice doing, as well as a language experience writing activity to share what it is like to have mice for class pets!

The Mice Use Their Senses

Preparation

Display five mice faces (pattern page 70) on wall, chalkboard, or bulletin board.

Label each and include an arrow pointing to the sense on the mouse's face. Note: For FEEL, use a mouse hand from the bulletin board patterns (page 72). Under each mouse hang paper for writing student responses as you ask the questions below.

See   Hear   Smell   Taste   Touch/Feel

Sense Questions

Use these questions with the SEE and HEAR activities, pages 9-11.

SEE   What did the Town Mouse see on the country walk?
What did the Town Mouse see the Country Mouse baking in the country kitchen?
What did the Country Mouse see when they arrived in the town?
What did the Country Mouse see in the living room and bedroom of the Town Mouse?
Who did the mice see when they were eating in the dining room?

HEAR   What did the Country Mouse hear the Town Mouse tell him at the dinner table in the country?
What sound did the Country Mouse become frightened by when they were in the town street?
What did the Country Mouse hear in the living room?
What different sounds did the mice hear while they were on the dining room table?
What sound was the Country Mouse making while he was walking back to his log home?

Use these questions with the SMELL and TASTE activities, pages 12-13.

SMELL   What did the Town Mouse smell cooking in the country kitchen?
What foods did the Country Mouse smell on the dining room table?
What did the Country Mouse smell in his mug when he was back in his log home?

TASTE   What did the Town Mouse taste at his country dinner?
What did the Country Mouse taste at his town dinner?
What did the Country Mouse taste when he got back to his log home at the end of the story?

Use these questions with the FEELING and FEELINGS activities, pages 14-16.

TOUCH/FEEL   When the mice went for a walk in the country, what things did they touch and feel?
What were some things that the Country Mouse could touch in the town?

Extension

Reproduce mouse face (page 70) and hats (page 17) onto heavy paper. Cut out eye holes, glue on hat of choice, and attach craft stick to chin to make a mouse mask. Use the masks in one or more of the following ways:

1. Students may give each other directions such as, "Point to what the mouse uses to smell ."

2. Have the students re-enact the story by pretending they are the Town and Country Mice.

3. Name a specific sense, and have the students act out a part in the story when that sense was used.

8

See and Hear

Younger students need more mobility than most. As adults we often forget about this! Sitting for long periods of time can even dull a child's senses, thus curbing the greatest possible learning potential. The activity below is designed to allow students to gain mobility, yet meet the objectives desired.

Lesson

Open the lesson by saying, ''To see we use our eyes; to hear we use our ears. Let's find out all of the things that the two mice saw and heard in the story.'' Guide the students back through the text and illustrations of *The Town Mouse and the Country Mouse*, stopping on each page to identify things that the mice saw and heard. Use the SEE and HEAR mice described on page 8 to list them. Discuss each item seen/heard briefly, reinforcing the concept that the mice used their ears to hear, their eyes to see.

Activity

To play the See and Hear Classifying Game reproduce the see and hear cards on page 10 so that, when distributed, the students will have an equal number of see cards and hear cards. (Example: 26 students=13 see cards, 13 hear cards.) Pass out the cards, face down, one per student. Explain the game by telling the students that they are going to be getting up and moving around the room until they find people holding the same kind of cards. Explain that the things on the HEAR cards can make noises. The things on the SEE cards usually do not. The HEAR cards have words on them for the noises the pictured object makes.

Designate an area in the room for each group to meet (i.e., ''SEE cards meet by the door, HEAR cards meet by the teacher's desk'').

The signal to begin the game will be a SEEING signal (teacher nodding head). The signal to end the game will be a hearing signal (blowing a whistle). When the whistle is blown, the groups face each other, showing their cards. As a class, decide if each group has classified (the definition of classified is ''putting things together that go together'') their cards correctly. Allow student input in this evaluation to check their understanding of the concepts presented.

See Cards   # Hear Cards

Name_____

My Eyes, My Ears

My Ears

Does it sound loud or soft?
Mark the box.
Color the pictures.

HEAR	LOUD	SOFT

My Eyes

Would you look up or down?
Mark the box.
Color the pictures.

LOOK	UP	DOWN

Smell and Taste

Students need to be able to think critically. This lesson's activity is designed to force students to make a guess (hypothesis) based on what they believe to be correct by their own prior knowledge and/or logical ideas of what they will be encountering.

Lesson

Say, "We use our nose to smell and our tongue and mouth to taste. Mice have a good sense of smell and taste. A mouse cannot see very well so it has to depend on its other senses. A mouse can smell food from far away. He doesn't need to see it to know what kind of food it is. A mouse likes to taste a lot of things that we would not think taste very good, like leather boots, old rags, paste and wood."

Reread *The Town Mouse and the Country Mouse* to find the things the mice smelled and tasted. Use the SMELL and TASTE mice described on page 8 to list them.

Activity 1

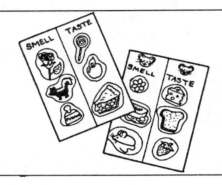
Provide each student with a piece of paper that has been divided in half. Have students write SMELL on one side and TASTE on the other. Pass out magazines, and have students cut out pictures that would be appropriate for each sense and paste them on the correct side. They may find that many things fall in both categories, so they will have to decide where they would like to place the item. Display finished work.

Activity 2

You will need: mice masks (how to's on page 8), peanut butter (in a non-see-through covered container), crackers, knife.

Steps:

1. Write the activity question on the board—Can you smell as well as a mouse? Allow each student to write yes or no around the question.

2. Pass out mice masks and ask the entire class to stand near the back of the classroom and pretend they are mice. You stand at the farthest possible point away from the students. Remove the lid of the "disguised" peanut butter. Tell the students that a mouse would be able to smell what is in the container from the distance that they are standing away from you. See if anyone can smell and tell what is in the container. Move two steps closer and ask if anyone can smell what is in it now. Continue until you get relatively close to the students and someone can finally state that they can smell peanut butter!

3. Have the class put down their mouse masks and look at the hypothesis question on the board. What was the correct answer? No, we cannot smell as well as a mouse.

4. When a mouse smells something as good as peanut butter it would definitely go and taste it! Put a small amount of peanut butter onto each cracker and allow the students to taste the peanut butter treat. Ask the students to share how the peanut butter and cracker tasted.

A Smell and Taste Experience

You will need: small paper nut cups (one per student), flower pattern, colored paper, cotton balls, peppermint candies (one per student), glue, scissors, peppermint extract

Steps:

1. Place one peppermint candy in each paper cup; set aside.

2. Use flower pattern to cut out one flower per student from construction paper.

3. Glue cotton ball to center of paper flowers.

4. Place a drop of peppermint extract onto each cotton ball.

5. Place a flower on top of each paper cup.

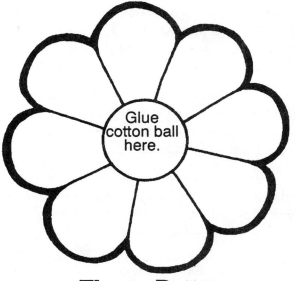

Glue cotton ball here.

Flower Pattern

Experience:

1. Explain that we use our nose to smell with, and our tongue and mouth to taste with. Have students point to their nose and take a deep breath. Have students point to their mouth and tongue and pretend they are chewing on a piece of bubble gum.

2. Ask the students to place their hands behind their back so that they will not be tempted to use them! Place a paper flower cup in front of each student.

3. Tell them that they will have to guess what kind of flower it is by using their nose. When you count to three, they are to put their nose close to the cotton ball and take a deep breath and smell the fragrance. Ask them to tell what they smelled. List their responses on chart paper.

4. Now ask them to close their eyes tightly. No peeking! Tell them to take their hands from behind their backs and lift off the flower to feel what is in the cup. Then they should put the treat in their mouth and taste it. After they taste, allow students to tell what they tasted. Put these responses on another chart.

5. Show the jar of peppermint extract and a piece of peppermint candy. Explain that these were what you used to tell their nose and mouth that they were smelling and tasting a sweet peppermint treat!

Feeling and Feelings

Students gain the highest retention when they have been able to experience a concept by seeing, hearing, doing, and using (synthesis). Encourage students to display their finished activity (page 15) on their refrigerator and daily change the information sheet. Instant synthesis!

Lesson

This lesson has been divided into four parts. Part one covers the sense of FEEL (touch). Part two covers the sense of FEELING (emotion). Parts three and four COMBINE the two.

Part One

Display a box of toys which display different textures, weights, and sizes. Call on a student to come up and choose a toy. Allow the student to tell the class how the toy feels. Encourage expressive language. (Example: A stuffed bear..."big, furry, soft, cuddly, smushy, light and lumpy") Continue until all toys have been felt. (Note: You do not have to have students feel with their hands. Have a student use his toes, another his face, and another the skin on his arm.)

Part Two

Display pictures or posters showing people expressing different feelings. Introduce each by sharing the emotion word that describes the picture. Then have students share their own experiences with the emotion.

(Example: With a picture of a child looking scared, ask students to share a time when they have been scared. Continue in this manner with the rest of the emotion pictures.)

Part Three

Prepare two small paper bags ahead of time by placing a fuzzy stuffed animal into BAG ONE and a plastic bag of well-cooked macaroni noodles in BAG TWO. Set aside. Begin part three by telling the students that sometimes when we feel by touching, it can make us have a certain feeling (emotion). Place BAG ONE and BAG TWO on a table. Ask a student to come up and feel with their fingers what is in BAG ONE and share with the class what emotion it makes them have. Because it is soft and fuzzy, possible answers may be warm, cozy, comfortable...like a special hug or slipping into a warm bed at night. Ask a student to come up and use their fingers to feel what is in BAG TWO. Instant emotion! Reinforce that sometimes when we feel with our skin it makes us have a certain emotional feeling.

Feeling and Feelings *(cont.)*

Part Four

Review the story *The Town Mouse and the Country Mouse*, to see if there were any times that the mice felt something with a touch that caused them to have a special feeling (emotion); for example, when they cooled their feet in the river, they had certain feelings. Use the TOUCH/FEEL mouse described on page 8 to list them.

Activity

Feeling Magnets

You will need: Feeling cards (below; one pair for each child), cardboard (2'' x 2''; two per student), scissors, glue, crayons, magnetic strips (available in craft stores; cut two 1'' strips per child), Touch and Emotion sheet page 16

Steps:

1. Pass out a pair of feeling cards (below) to each student. Allow students to color and cut out each card.

2. Pass out cardboard (two per student) and glue.

3. Glue feeling cards onto cardboard pieces. Allow to dry thoroughly.

4. Attach a magnet on the back of the cardboard piece.

5. Provide each student with a copy of page 16. Explain that they are to take their magnets home and place them on a metal surface (e.g., the refrigerator). Each day, they are to draw a picture and put it under the appropriate feeling card. Encourage them to draw a new picture each day to show that what we touch and how we feel inside can change often.

Touch

Emotion

Touch and Emotion

Touch
To feel using your skin

*See suggested activity page 15.

The word FEEL can mean two different things.

Emotion
To feel in your heart

Town and Country Hats

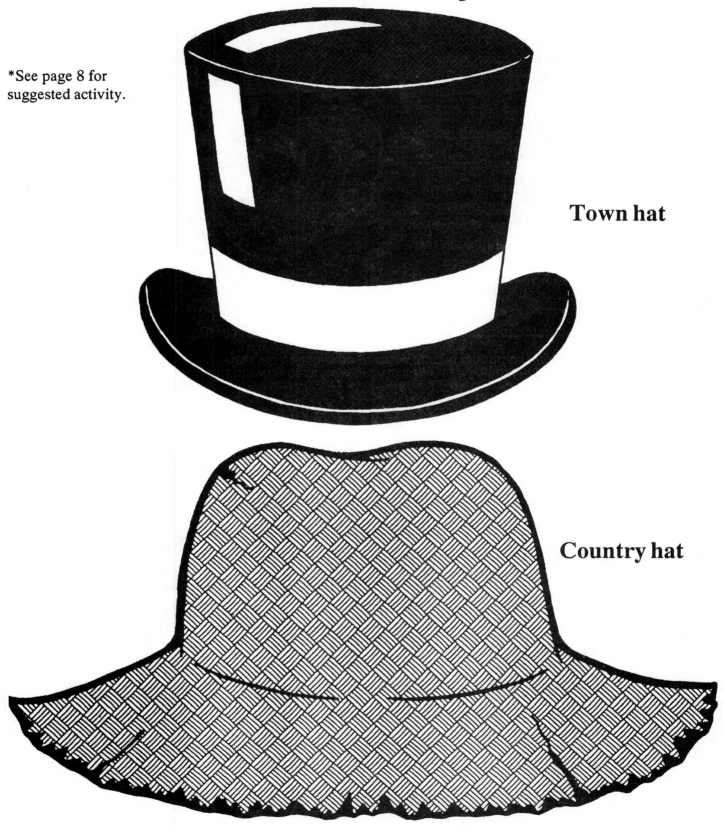

*See page 8 for suggested activity.

Town hat

Country hat

The Little Red Hen

Suggested version: retold and illustrated by Paul Galdone

Summary

Due to her three housemates' laziness, the little red hen is left to do all the work from cooking the meals to hoeing the garden. One day, she finds some grains of wheat. We follow her sequential adventures through planting, tending, harvesting, processing, and baking a delicious wheat cake. Whenever she asks for help, she hears a unanimous, "Not I!" However, when her wheat cake is ready to eat, the three housemates are ready to help. The little red hen reminds them of all she did by herself to create the cake, so she plans to enjoy it by herself, too! Learning this lesson, the cat, dog, and mouse decide to change their ways and become househelpers.

This humorous traditional story is perfect for introducing and reinforcing concepts of classification and sequencing, as well as reviewing the five senses. The rich vocabulary that Mr. Galdone uses will surely increase the verbal and/or written vocabulary of your students.

Sample Plan

Day I

- Discuss wheat and wheat products (page 19)
- Chart chores and problems (page 19)
- Write "My Chore Report" (page 45)
- Introduce the little red hen with paper plate project (page 39)
- Show and discuss book cover
- Discuss Make-Believe vs. Real (use page 47)
- Read *The Little Red Hen*
- Use sentence strips (pages 21-23)

Day II

- Introduce selected vocabulary from page 24.
- Reread story, listening for vocabulary words
- Use sentence strips to retell story
- Sort and classify grains (page 25)
- Make paper bag puppets (pages 26-29)
- Make plays in teams (page 20)

Day III

- Study sequencing (page 30)
- Reread *The Little Red Hen*, noting the sequence from grain to cake.

- Do Sequencing Activity (page 30)
- Complete "From Grain to Cake" (page 31)
- Review five senses with classification activity (pages 32-34)

Day IV

- Use Math Story Background (pages 50-51)
- Study real chickens (pages 35-37)
- Visit a chicken farm and/or hatch eggs.
- Do "On an Adventure" activity (page 44)

Day V

- Culminating Activity: Bake wheat cake (recipe, page 62)
- Make class Big Book "The Helpful Housemates" (page 46)

Overview of Activities

SETTING THE STAGE

1. Set the mood by creating curiosity about what wheat is and what it is used for. Bring in five to ten examples of wheat products (wheat muffins, wheat cereals, granola, breads, bagels, crackers). Discuss and display.

2. The little red hen has a big problem...no one to help her with the chores! Display a chart labeled CHORES. Allow students to name chores they are responsible for at home. List them on the chart. Explain that in the story the little red hen's problem was due to lazy housemates. Display a chart labeled PROBLEMS. Allow students to share some of their own problems. Ask how these problems make them feel (emotions).

3. Tape record the story. Use parent helpers to play the different voice roles. You will need a voice for the little red hen, the cat, the dog, and the mouse. Place recorder and tape in listening area with a copy of the book. After you have read the story to the class, allow students to listen to the recording.

4. Show the cover of *The Little Red Hen*. Ask questions like: What is she doing? Is this a real or imaginary chicken? How do you know? Review the five senses by asking children to point to the body parts the little red hen uses for seeing, hearing (small hole on side of head), smelling (nostrils on top of beak), tasting, and touching. Compare them with a human body.

5. Make paper plate little red hens (page 39).

ENJOYING THE BOOK

1. Read *The Little Red Hen* aloud to the class.

2. Reread the story, and have students join in on the repetitive, "Not I," and, "Then I will." Use the sentence strips on pages 21-23 to reinforce this vocabulary. The strips may be prepared for use in a pocket chart on a flannel board, or on a magnetic board. Students may "play" at matching what the character said with who said it.

3. After introducing your choice of vocabulary and/or spelling words (page 24), reread the story and have the students "cluck" every time they hear one of the introduced words. This not only reinforces the words, but reviews the sense of hearing.

4. Refer back to the page in the story where the little red hen discovers the wheat grains. Discuss the word "grain." (It is "the small, hard seed of any cereal plant," according to Webster's Dictionary.) Explain that there are other types of grains besides wheat grains. Display labeled clear plastic bags containing the following grains: oats, corn, rice, barley, and wheat. (Check grocery, feed, and pet stores; guinea pig or rodent food mixes may be used.) Have students describe how each grain looks and feels (using seeing and feeling senses).

Overview of Activities *(cont.)*

4. *(cont.)* Divide the class into teams of five or six students. Provide a sorting sheet (page 25) for each student. Have them color it, leaving the boxes uncolored. Place a bowl of mixed grains in the middle of each team. The team pours the grains out on the table and classifies them into the five grain groups. Provide glue, and allow students to classify the grains onto their worksheets. Keep the labeled bags visible as a resource for students to refer to if not certain of a specific grain's name. When worksheets are dry, display.

5. Divide the class into teams of five. Four students will play the roles of the characters in the story, and the fifth will be the narrator. Help students create their own puppets for a ''Little Red Hen Puppet Show.'' (Patterns are provided on pages 26-29 for paper bag puppets.) Have each team make their own background and practice their play. When all teams are ready, have a special ''class performance'' dress rehearsal, then permit each team to ''go on the road'' with their production and present it to another class or grade level.

6. Do Sequencing and Classifying Activities (pages 30-34).

EXTENDING THE BOOK

1. Study real chickens. Use pages 35-37.

2. A great adventure for extending the story would be to take a field trip to a local chicken farm. Many have guided tours through the various sections of the farm. If your students are lucky, maybe they will get to take home a real chicken feather! The five senses will be well-utilized on such an excursion.

3. Another exciting activity would be to incubate fertilized eggs and watch them hatch into fuzzy little chicks. Incubation takes approximately 21 days. Students can take on the ''chores'' to make certain that the incubator is at the correct temperature (skill: reading a thermometer), turning the eggs twice daily (responsibility), and finding homes for the chicks when they get old enough. Consult the Bibliography (page 79) for resource books on how to hatch fertilized eggs. Fuzzy new chicks are a ''touch'' and ''hear'' treat.

4. Before completing the culminating activity (page 63), have your students graph whether they think they will like the taste of the wheat cake they are going to make. Display the graph. After making, baking, and eating the cake, have the students put their response to tasting the wheat cake on a separate graph. Compare the two graphs. (Pattern for graphs, page 38.)

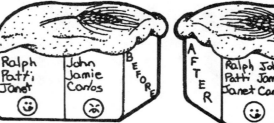

Sentence Strips

*See suggested activity page 19

Sentence Strips *(cont.)*

said the cat.

said the dog.

said the mouse.

Sentence Strips *(cont.)*

"Then I will,"

said the little

red hen.

Tab

Vocabulary Development

Paul Galdone's *The Little Red Hen* contains excellent enriching vocabulary. The words listed below can be used in three ways:

1. Oral Vocabulary Development (Speaking)

2. Written Vocabulary Development (Spelling)

3. Extended Vocabulary Development (Various words for a given concept)

ORAL	WRITTEN	EXTENDED
little poured red shining hen batter cozy oven house bowl cat delicious sleep strolled soft kitchen couch scampered dog beautiful nap eat sunny cried porch planted mouse tended snooze ripe chair built fireside crumb housework eager cooked helpers washed mixed swept sticks mended gathered raked cake mowed fine hoed flour grains grind wheat mill weeds cut ground	bowl cake cat dog eat flour grain hen house little mill oven red wheat	**Action Words** cooked built washed tended swept planted mended cried(yelled) raked scampered mowed strolled hoed poured grind mixed gathered **Descriptive Words** little red sunny soft cozy fine shining delicious beautiful eager **Animal Words** hen cat dog mouse **Compound Words** fireside housework

Sorting Grains

Name: _____

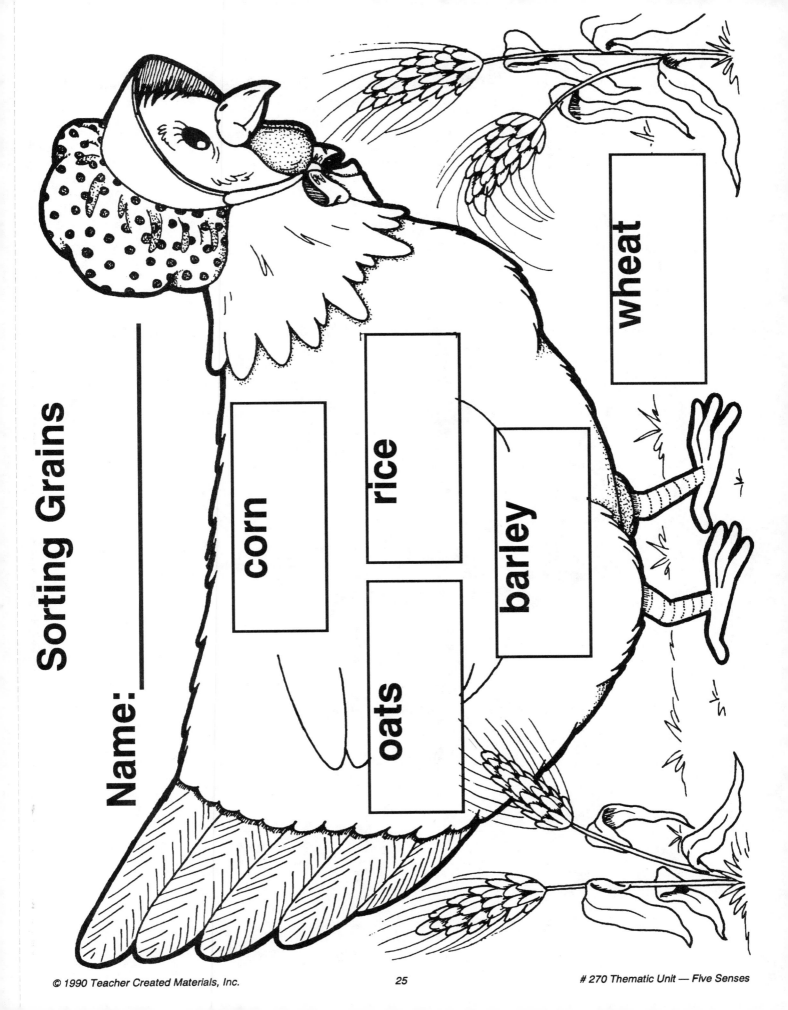

wheat

corn

rice

oats

barley

Little Red Hen Paper Bag Puppets

Glue to flap of lunch-size
paper bag.

Glue under bag flap.

Mouse Paper Bag Puppet

Glue to flap of lunch-size paper bag.

Glue under bag flap.

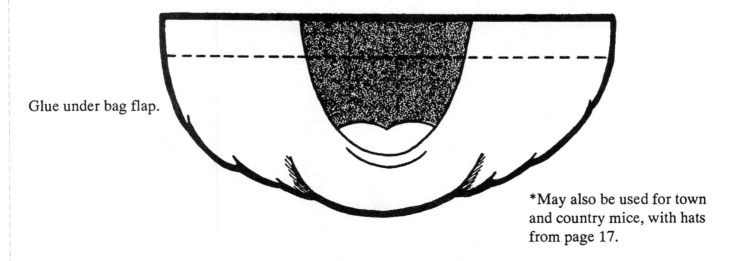

*May also be used for town and country mice, with hats from page 17.

Cat Paper Bag Puppet

Glue to flap of lunch-size paper bag.

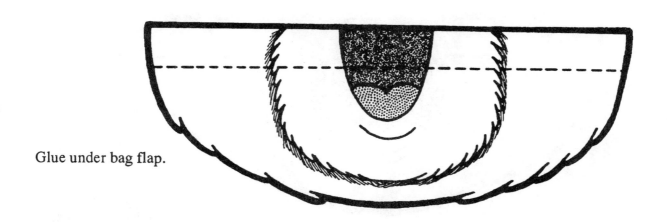

Glue under bag flap.

Dog Paper Bag Puppet

Glue to flap of lunch-size
paper bag.

Glue under bag flap.

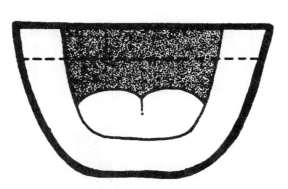

Sequencing

Note to teacher: When teaching your children a new skill such as sequencing, it helps to state the skill concept as a rule. For example: "Sequencing means...what comes first, what comes second, what comes third, and sometimes more!" As students are saying this rule, have them hold up one finger when saying "what comes first," two fingers for "what comes second," and three fingers for "what comes third?" As they are saying, "sometimes more," have them continue to hold up one more finger (sequentially) until they have all ten fingers open in the air. This form of "rule-stating" and "actions" helps the students to retain the concept through visual (looking at fingers) as well as an auditory (speaking and hearing) mode.

Lesson

Enact a little "sequencing task" for your students. Ask them to watch carefully what you are doing. Encourage them to use their sense of sight. Tell them that you will be asking them to repeat the order in which you completed the task. (Sample tasks: Putting on your shoe and tying it; writing a note, placing it in an envelope, and sealing it; walking to your desk, getting a pencil, then walking back to the point at which you began.) After you complete the task, have students verbally tell you what you did. Explain that you completed the task in order. When things are done in a certain order, it is called sequencing. Reread the story. Have the students "discover" the sequence of how the wheat seeds grew into wheat stalks and then were made into the wheat cake. Hand out the worksheet on page 31. As a group, complete the worksheet. State the rule for sequencing that was given in the Note to Teacher. Show how the growing of wheat is an example of "...sometimes more!" Display finished worksheets.

Activity

Divide the class into teams of two. Allow each person to complete their own "sequencing tasks" while their partner watches carefully. After completing the task, the partner tells in order what was done. After both partners have had a turn, provide white paper, pencils, and crayons, and allow partners to illustrate and label (placing the numbers 1,2,3,4... next to the illustrations). Advanced students may add simple sentences. Let the teams share and display their sequencing task pictures.

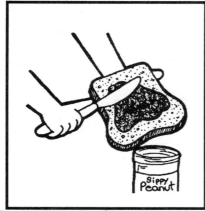
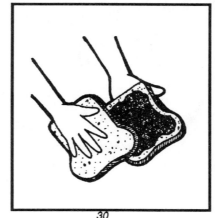

From Grain to Cake

1. Color the pictures.
2. Cut them out.
3. Put in order.
4. Glue into a booklet.
5. Write or tell the story.

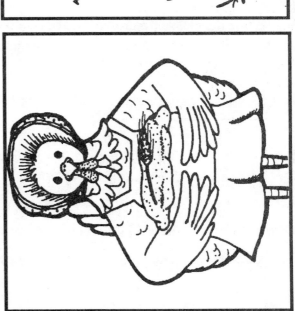

*Teacher should provide each student with a blank 8-page booklet. The front is the cover. Pictures are glued inside, one per page.

31

Classification

This lesson has been designed to teach classification as well as to provide an excellent opportunity to review the five senses.

Lesson

Place a brown lunch sack and a backpack on a table. Have students tell you what each "bag" is used for. Display the following real items: a pencil, orange, sandwich, notebook, cookies, crayon box, thermos or carton of milk, and a library book. Tell the class that you want them to classify these items. State: "Classifying means putting things together that go together." (As they are stating the skill "rule," have the students use their hands to show separating things in the air.) Call on various students to classify each of the items on the table into the correct sack. When completed, check by taking out the contents of each bag and asking if the items in the particular sack go together. Once you feel that the students have mastered the concept, review the five senses by describing how each item looks and how it might sound, smell, taste, and feel. Enjoy the funny answers!

Activity

Preparation:

- Divide the class into groups of 3 or 4.
- For each group have the following available:
  1. five index cards labeled with the senses—SEE, HEAR, SMELL, TASTE, TOUCH.
  2. a set of Sense Picture Cards (pages 33-34) that have been colored, cut apart, and laminated.

Procedure:

Have students sort the picture cards by placing them with the index card that names the sense they represent. You may wish to practice as a class first.

Extension:

Direct students to draw additional picture cards to be added to the activity.

This game may be stored in a manila envelope and used as a center activity.

Sense Picture Cards

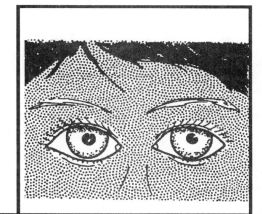

*See suggested activity, page 32.

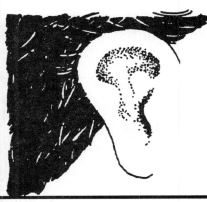  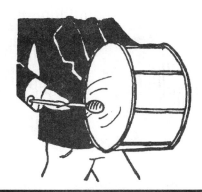

Sense Picture Cards (cont.)

*See suggested activity, page 32.

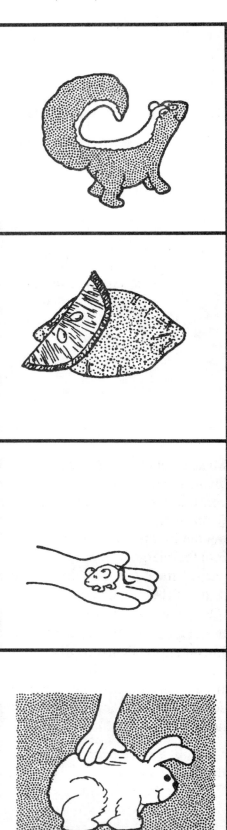

Real Chickens

An excellent extension activity for *The Little Red Hen* is to learn about real chickens. This will help students begin to distinguish between real and make-believe, fact and fantasy, nonfiction and fiction. (Use page 47 for practice making this distinction.) This lesson focuses on the life cycle of a hen.

Lesson

- Discuss the names of chicken family members—male=rooster, female=hen, babies=chicks. Use page 36 to reinforce this vocabulary. Children may wish to draw and label their own chicken families.

- Reread *The Little Red Hen* noting all the jobs for which the little red hen is responsible. List them on chart paper. Ask the students if the jobs are real or make-believe work for a hen. Make a second chart of things real hens might do.

- Discuss the life cycle of a hen: Eggs are laid and kept warm by a hen. Chicks hatch from fertilized eggs. The chicks learn to eat so they can grow. Some of the chicks grow up to be hens who will lay eggs to start the cycle all over again. Extension: Give and/or elicit examples of other life cycles; e.g., butterfly, frog, human, etc.

- Include the five senses in your discussion. What sounds do chickens make? How do they look (size, colors, body parts, etc.)? What foods do chickens like to taste? How do baby chicks feel when you touch them? etc.

Activity

Make Cycle Circles. Cut an 18" (45 cm) diameter circle from 18" x 24" (45 x 60 cm) construction paper, and reproduce page 37 for each student. Have them color and cut out the four pictures. Tell the students to fold their large paper circle into four equal parts. Direct them to place the pictures in sequential order, one picture per section. (Do not let them paste the pictures down until you have checked their cycle first!) Encourage students to write a sentence in each section describing what is happening. If your students cannot write their own sentences, have them dictate to you or a helper. Display the completed products.

Last, but not least, have the students state the rule of a cycle. "A cycle is what comes first, second, third, and fourth... over and over again!" (Hand movement is a clenched fist with extended index finger, rotating in a circular motion.)

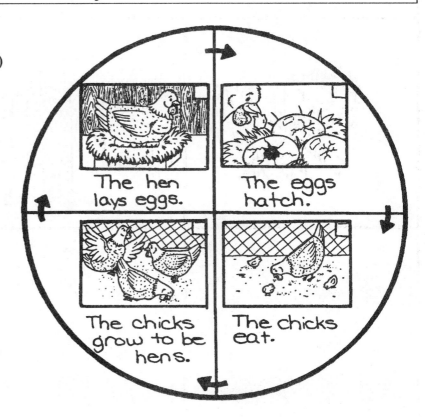

The hen lays eggs.

The eggs hatch.

The chicks grow to be hens.

The chicks eat.

Chicken Family Sounds

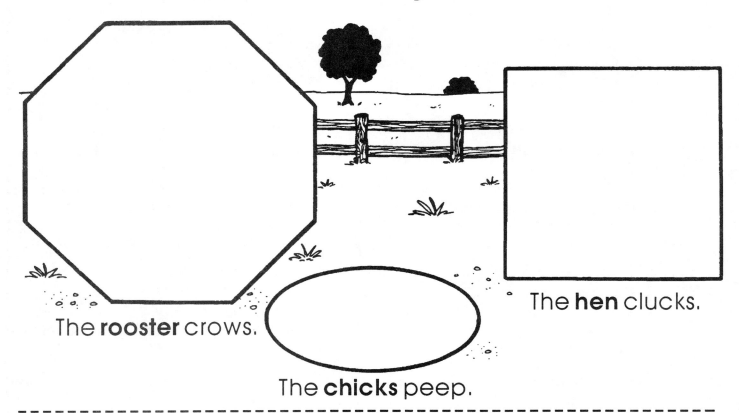

The **rooster** crows.

The **chicks** peep.

The **hen** clucks.

---

1. Color.

2. Cut.

3. Paste.

Name _____

Life Cycle of a Hen

Color, cut out, and put in the correct order on a cycle circle.

Graph Pattern

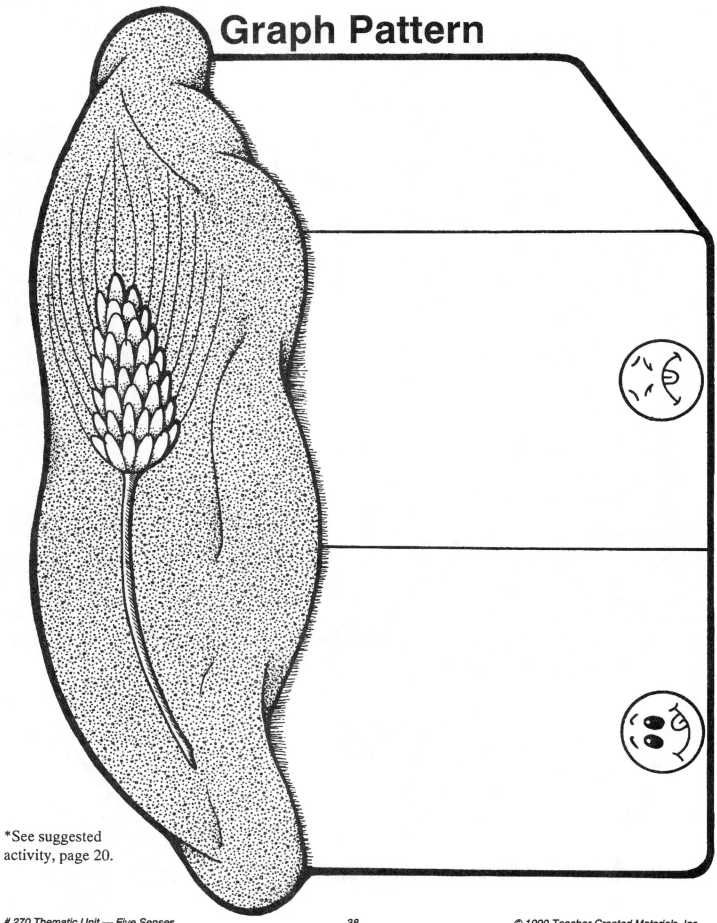

*See suggested
activity, page 20.

Paper Plate Little Red Hen

1. Color.

2. Cut out.

3. Paste onto dessert size paper plate. Put tools **under** wing.

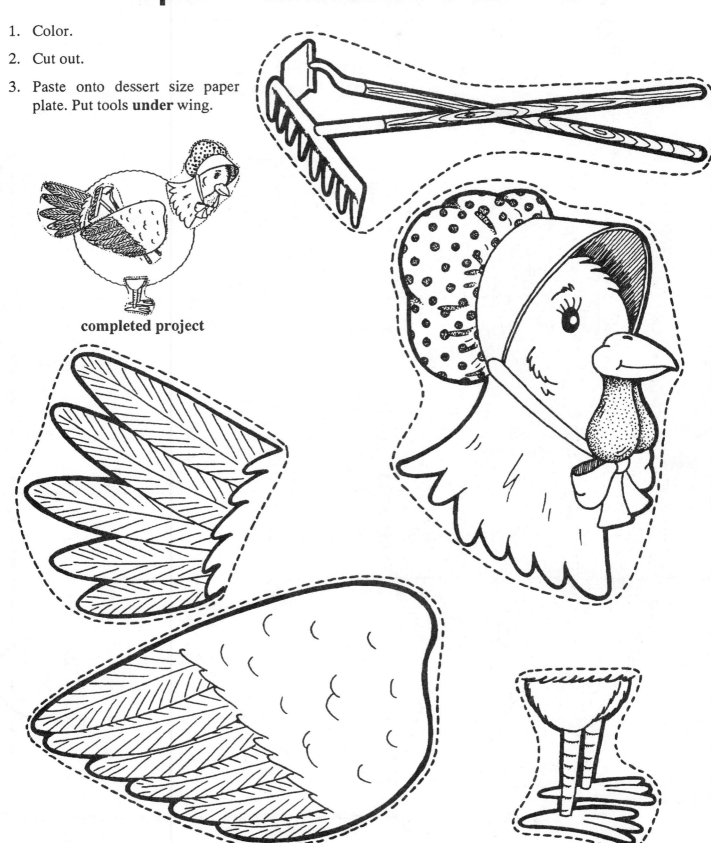

completed project

The Little Red Hen Puzzle

1. Cut.   2. Sequence.   3. Glue onto a piece of paper.   4. Color.

Who will help me
cut the wheat?

Who will help me
bake this cake?

Who will help me
plant the wheat?

Who will help me eat this cake?

**THE LITTLE RED
HEN'S QUESTIONS**

Who will help me
grind the wheat?

Poetry

My Sense Poem

This is a simplified version of "free style" poetry. The beginning of the poem will be the same for everyone, but the additions will be each student's own. After they write the poem on large paper (or use the form on page 42), allow the students to illustrate it.

Variations: Make similar poems for the other senses using these beginnings:

There are so many,

I can hardly tell

Everything I taste and smell.

I'd like to show you very much

All the things I'd like to touch.

Mother Goose

Use familiar rhymes like "Simple Simon" and "Little Tommy Tucker" which refer to the senses. "Bow-Wow" (below) is a great "hearing" poem.

Bow-Wow

Bow-wow says the dog,

   Mew, mew says the cat,

Grunt, grunt goes the hog,

   And squeak goes the rat.

Whoo-oo says the owl,

   Caw, caw says the crow,

Quack, quack says the duck,

   And what cuckoos say, you know.

So with cuckoos and owls,

   With rats and with dogs,

With ducks and with crows

   With cats and with hogs,

A fine song I have made,

   To please you, my dear;

And if it's well-sung,

   'Twill be charming to hear.

The Mother Goose rhyme, "The Little Mouse" could have been written about the town mouse.

The Mother Goose poems "The Red Hen" and "The Clever Hen" can easily be used with the activities for *The Little Red Hen.*

My Sense Poem

by _____

Every day is new to me.

I take time to hear and see!

I see...   **I hear...**

_____   _____

_____   _____

_____   _____

42

Language and Writing Experiences

Note to Teacher: To gain the maximum writing potential from your students, enlist the help of volunteers or aides during these language experiences.

Five Senses Accordion Book

To make an accordion book, fold four 12" x 18" pieces of colored paper in half. Tape "middle" edges to form accordion pages. Completed books can be folded for easy storage. To complete the "My Five Senses" accordion book, have students write the sentences as shown below, then illustrate them. For younger students, write the text and allow them to illustrate.

Jelly Jiggle Squares

To prepare for this writing experience you will need to make the following recipe:

Ingredients:

  4 pkgs. (3 oz. each) (90 g) flavored gelatin
  2 1/2 cups (750 mL) boiling water
  1 pkg. unflavored gelatin

Directions:

1. Pour the four packages of flavored gelatin into a large bowl.

2. Add the package of unflavored gelatin.

3. Add the boiling water. Stir until mixture is completely dissolved.

4. Pour into pan. Chill in refrigerator at least four hours. Cut into squares, or use cookie cutters to make jiggle shapes.

For the writing activity, give each student a jiggle square or shape. Ask them to smell, then taste their jiggles. After they eat them, allow them to write about their smelling and tasting experience, individually or as a class.

When I Feel, I Feel...

Using the same principle as with the accordion book (above) have students write how they feel (feeling) when they feel (touch) certain items. Encourage them to try to express different feelings, such as happy, sad, scared, worried, puzzled, giggly.

Language and Writing Experiences

(cont.)

My Favorite Sensation Station

After students have completed all of the Sensation Stations (Culminating Activity, pages 63-67), have them write about and illustrate their favorite station. When all writings are completed, make a Sensation Station book; classify the writings by "stations" so that there will be five chapters. Bind the Sensation Station book and display it for all to read.

Paper Hen Story

Duplicate a little red hen pattern (page 39) for each student onto white construction paper. Have students put together the little red hen by pasting pieces onto a dessert-size plate (refer to small picture of completed hen on page 39). Then students may write about one of the following topics: the sequence of events in the story, *The Little Red Hen*, a real or make-believe hen, their favorite part of the story, or how they put their paper hen together.

Display the completed stories and little red hens.

On An Adventure...

To encourage the use of prepositional phrases, display a chart with the following words already written:

On An Adventure

On the way to ____ the Little Red Hen
went over the _____ to smell _____,
under a _____ to see a _____,
behind a _____ to hear the _____,
through a _____ to touch a _____,
into the _____ to feel _____.
At the end of her adventure the Little Red Hen
felt _____!

As a class, build a story by filling in the blanks. Then provide a piece of writing paper and allow students to copy the story frame and fill in the blanks with their own ideas. Note: If students are too young to copy the words, hand out pre-written copies and fill in blanks for students as they orally share their ideas. Provide each student with an additional piece of blank paper and have them illustrate their story. Display on a bulletin board or in the hallway for all to read and enjoy!

Language and Writing Experiences
(cont.)

My Chore Report

Refer to the list of jobs for which the little red hen was responsible. Ask again if these are jobs that a real hen would do. Then ask the students to share what chores they are responsible for at home. Have them write a Chore Report, telling the sequence of tasks for their chore. After students are finished with the writing process, have them switch reports with a classmate to illustrate doing the chore. When illustrations are complete, have students return the Chore Reports to the original authors. Everyone checks to see if the illustrations match the sequencing of the chore. Note: If students are too young to write, allow them to dictate their report. They can then illustrate their own Chore Report.

Is, Is Not Book

After discussing foods that are made from wheat, allow students to write an Is, Is Not Book by working in teams of two. Each team gets eight sheets of writing paper and a few magazines. A team is to work together to find eight pictures (four items made from wheat products and four items that are not). After they cut out the eight pictures, they paste them on paper alternating is, is not pictures. The team then writes or dictates complete sentences under each picture to form the written text for the book. When a team has completed all eight sentences, provide construction paper to make a cover. Staple cover and pages together, and have teams read their finished writing project to their classmates. Display books for all to read during free or planned reading times.

Make a Class Big Book

1. Review the story, *The Little Red Hen*, emphasizing the chores the little red hen was responsible for. Discuss the ending in depth. Explain that the class will be extending the story by writing a Big Book called *The Helpful Housemates*. The story will be about the housemates (dog, cat, mouse) completing chores around the house.

2. Discuss the following as a pre-writing activity:
   - The chores that students do at their houses that can be adapted for the three animals
   - Sequencing how to do the chores that the animals will be completing
   - What the little red hen will be doing while the housemates are helping
   - The need for their illustrations to match the text of the story

3. List possibilities and vote to choose six chores (two per animal) that the housemates can complete. Elicit vocabulary words pertaining to each chore (for example: dusting—mop, cloth, rub, spray, shiny, dirty; making beds—sheets, blankets, tuck around, cover, fluff, pillows, bed).

4. As a class, write a story out in rough draft form onto large chart paper. Edit it as a class. Does it have a beginning, a middle, and an ending? Does it make sense?

5. At this time, take a break and allow students to complete other tasks. While they are busy (or have gone home for the day), write the text of the Big Book on large chart paper pages. (Note: Do not overload a page with too much text. If it is too complicated, it will be hard for the children to illustrate accurately.)

6. When students return for the second half of the activity, gather them around to read each of the Big Book pages. (Note: During this time, the pages are not bound together because they still need to be illustrated!) Explain that in teams of two or three they will cooperate to illustrate the text. They should plan and draw out pictures with a pencil first. Then with teacher or parent approval, they color their illustrations.

7. Compile completed pages in sequential order. Add a title page in the front and an additional page in the back with the words THE END on it. Bind the Big Book together with string, rings, or staples.

8. Read the newly created Big Book, *The Helpful Housemates*, as a class. For an extension, have students go in small teams to other classrooms to share their Big Book. Add the Big Book to the class library for all to read!

46

Name_____ Language Arts

Make-Believe or Real

Look at these pictures from storybooks. If the story is make-believe, write MB in the box. If it is real, write R. Color the pictures.

Hear Me, See Me Matching Game

Supplies needed: Tape recorder; pre-taped sounds (suggestions below); appropriate pictures to match sounds recorded (you may use pages 10 and 49); construction paper or tagboard; scissors; black marking pen; glue; masking tape

Assembling game:

1. Choose 5 to 10 sounds. Record these sounds onto a cassette tape. Leave a blank "sound space" in between each sound. For example:

people talking	**dogs barking**	**guitar playing**	**footsteps**
bells ringing	**sirens**	**rain falling**	**pots/pans banging**
clock ticking	**birds singing**	**telephone ringing**	**typewriter typing**

2. Find pictures that match the sounds you have recorded. (Or, use pictures from pages 10 and 49.) Mount them onto construction paper or tagboard.

3. On strips of 3" x 12" paper, write the name of the object(s) making the recorded sounds.

To Play:

1. Place the pictures on a chalkboard ledge or tape to the chalkboard. Have students come and sit on the floor near the board. Discuss what they see in each picture.

2. Turn on the tape recorder so that they can hear the first sound. Ask them to tell you what picture the sound matches. When they have identified the correct picture, tape the corresponding strip with word text next to the picture and read it together. (For example: The sound on the recorder is of a clock ticking. When the students identify the correct picture, place the word strip "clock ticking" next to the picture.) Repeat with the remaining sounds.

Sound Picture Cards

*See activity, page 48. (Hear Cards from page 10 may also be used.)

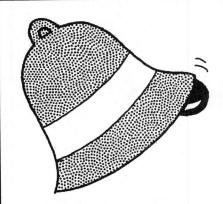

270 Thematic Unit — Five Senses

Math Story Background

Give each student a math story background to put together. (Glue right edge of picture on this page on top of Tab A on page 51). They may color the pictures with crayons, markers, or paints. Glue to tagboard and laminate for more durability.

Attach on top of Tab A.

50

Using the Math Story Background

Provide each student with counters/markers–beans, buttons, dry macaroni, etc. As you relate a math story-problem, students manipulate their counters accordingly. For example: "There are five mice in the well. One jumped out and scampered to the barn. How many are left in the well?"

Tab A

Smells?

1. Put an X on the ones that smell bad to you.

2. Color the ones that smell good to you.

Tongue Teaser

Supplies needed: Oranges and grapefruits; knife; small paper plates (2 per student); plastic forks (1 per student); experiment report (optional)

Question: If you hold your nose to stop your sense of smell, can you still taste?

Hypothesis:
(check one)

☐ Yes, I can still taste.
☐ No, I cannot still taste.

Experiment:

Place a section of grapefruit and section of orange on separate paper plates (one set per student). Divide students into pairs. Partner A holds his own nose and closes his eyes while Partner B uses a fork to put one of the two pieces of fruit into Partner's A mouth. Partner A chews and swallows the fruit without peeking! Continue the process with the second piece of fruit (still holding nose). Partner A then tries to tell Partner B which was the first fruit he was given, and which one was the second. (Partner A will have to guess because when he holds his nose he is cutting off the flow of air leading to the "olfactory receptors" [smelling sensors] inside his nose, which help the taste buds realize what they are eating!) Now, partner B holds his own nose and closes his eyes and is given his fruit by Partner A. After each partner has shared the experience of eating the fruit with their nose and eyes closed, allow them to have two new pieces of fruit. They can eat them without closing their nose to understand how important our "nose sensors" are, and that our two senses, smell and taste, work together just like the partners did to complete this experiment!

If using the form below, allow each team to complete it together.

Experiment Report by _____ **and** _____

1. Could you tell which piece was the orange and which piece was the grapefruit:

   with your nose pinched? Yes _____ No _____

   with your nose not pinched? Yes _____ No _____

2. Was your hypothesis correct?

   Partner A: Yes _____ No _____ Partner B: Yes _____ No _____

3. What did you learn? _____

A Three "S" Party

Sweet	Sour	Salty
candy sugar cube fruit punch chocolate fruit doughnuts cupcake with frosting	lemons sour candies grapefruit vinegar	pretzels potato chips grains of salt crackers beef jerky peanuts pickles

1. Give each student a plate with a food from each of the three S categories above.

2. Write the three descriptive words on the board: SWEET, SOUR, SALTY. Discuss the words briefly.

3. Have the students try their three food examples and talk to a neighbor around them to decide how they would classify the foods that they have tasted into the three categories.

4. Ask the students to tell you how they would classify each food item and then to write the food names under the correct descriptive word.

5. Pass out another plate to each student containing three new samples of food (one from each category) and repeat steps three and four.

Extension: Provide paper and have the students chart their foods, noting taste, texture, and color.

Example:

Food	Taste	Texture	Color
pretzel	salty	bumpy	brown and white
candy cane	sweet	smooth and curvy	white and red
lemon	sour	mushy	yellow

Touch and Feel Cooperative Game

Making Game Cards

You will need: Page 56 reproduced onto heavy paper (1 for every 2 students); marker; scissors; glue; textured materials (two of the same items for each texture given below)

ROUGH —sandpaper, thin scouring pad

SMOOTH —aluminum foil, paper, ribbon

BUMPY — wallpaper, corrugated cardboard

HARD — wood, metal, macaroni pieces

SOFT — fabric, cotton balls, yarn

1. Cut out cards.

2. Glue like items onto 2 matching cards.

Note: For more cards, simply reproduce additional copies of page 56 and vary items placed on matching cards.

Playing "Touch and Feel"

You will need: game cards (directions above, one set per team); blindfold (one for each team of two players)

1. Divide the class into teams of two. Give each team a blindfold and a set of textured playing cards.

2. Blindfold a member of the team. Partner lays out cards (textured side up) in front of the blindfolded person.

3. The blindfolded player touches the cards and tries to make a match. When he has matched them all correctly, the players switch the blindfold to give the other team member a turn.

Variations:

1. Both team members are blindfolded and a third person lays out cards in front of them. They take turns feeling two cards at a time. If they feel the same (and have made a match), they may take the cards. (This is similar to the sighted "memory" game.)

2. Students use cards like they are playing "Go Fish;" both wear blindfolds.

Touch and Feel Cards

soft	soft
hard	hard
bumpy	bumpy
smooth	smooth
rough	rough

Animal Drums

Young children enjoy learning beats and rhythms. This activity will extend the concept of hearing, as well as develop the basic understanding of the world of music.

Materials

Empty cylindrical containers with lids (oatmeal cartons; coffee cans; ice cream cartons; etc.); scissors; glue; construction paper; crayons/markers

Construction

1. Cut paper to fit the size of the cylindrical container.

2. Student decorates paper with colorful animal pictures. (If incorporating the two stories in this unit, the animals could be a hen, mouse, dog, cat, horse, and bird).

3. Glue paper to the outside of the cylindrical container. Place lid on top of container.

Activities

1. Have the students sit cross-legged in a large circle, placing their animal drums in their laps. Tell them that they are going to play animal music melodies. On their drums you will want them to beat a soft sound if you say "mouse," a loud sound if you say "horse," and a medium sound if you say "hen." Start off with the animal of your choice, making sure that all students are on task. Then state a different animal and see who remembers to change their beat. Continue changing the animals, gradually changing animal beats at a faster rate. To make it more complicated, add more animal beats using different types of beats or beat patterns (slow-slow-fast/ slow-fast-slow-fast).

2. Take an animal march through the hallways or out on the playground, asking the students to beat their drums in a marching cadence (hard-hard-soft-soft-hard-hard-soft-soft) as you walk along.

3. Divide the class into teams of "animals." On flashcards list the different animals. Gather students into their teams and let them sit together on the floor. Flash a card, but do not read it aloud. Let the students read the word themselves, and if it is their animal group, they begin to beat their animal drums. In a few moments, show the next card. The new "animal" group should begin to beat their drums and the previous group should stop. (Note: If working with younger students, place pictures of the animals on the flashcards.)

Mood Music

In current times, young students are often not exposed to classical, jazz, Dixieland, and other types of quality music. Music causes feelings inside of us. By completing this activity, students will express through art how the music they are listening to makes them feel.

Materials

Tape recorder or record player; various types of quality music (most public libraries provide an excellent selection from which to borrow); plain paper; pencils; crayons; markers; water colors

Activity

1. Decide which medium the students will be using. (Note: It is fun to change the medium as you change the style of music.) Provide paper and the selected art materials for each student.

2. Ask the students to close their eyes. Tell them to pretend they are looking at a blank TV screen in their mind. You are going to play a certain type of music and you want them to listen carefully to the music. As they listen with eyes closed, tell them to ''look'' at their ''TV screen'' and see what kind of ''picture'' begins to form.

3. After playing the music for a few moments, whisper to the class that you want them to open their eyes and begin to draw the picture they saw on their ''TV screen.'' They are to do this without talking to anyone around them as they continue to listen to the music. When everyone has finished their drawing, turn off the music and allow each student to share their pictures and feelings with the rest of the class.

4. Continue as outlined in steps two through four using a different style of music. This may be done on several days.

Extension

After trying a few individual pictures, divide the class into teams of five or six and provide a large sheet of butcher paper. Play a new style of music. The team decides how the music sounds and draws a mural together. Display the music murals with the title and style of music used for their creation.

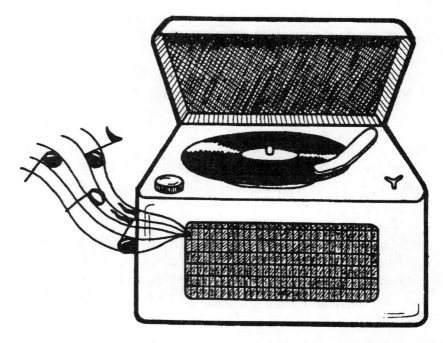

58

Textured T

Materials

Cardboard or oaktag, cut in a T shape; glue; black marker; various textured items such as: corrugated cardboard, fabrics, foil, sandpaper, yarn, string, macaroni shells, plastic packing materials, wood pieces, dried beans, seeds, and any other textured items you have available

Construction

1. Provide each student with an oaktag or cardboard T.

2. With the black marker, write the student's name on the bottom of the T as follows:

   Child's Name Textured T (Example: Sara's Textured T; Wes's Textured T)

3. Lay the textured items on a table or counter top. Instruct students to cut (or tear) and glue many different textured items onto their T.

4. When all students are done, have them trade their T so that others can feel the various combinations of textures assembled on the T's. Display.

Note:

Depending on the level of your students, it may be desirable to spend a little time on the definition of texture before you begin the art activity.

Non-Edible Recipes

(For Tactile Experiences)

Baking Clay

Ingredients:

8 cups (2L) flour;   2 cups (500 mL) salt;   3 cups (750 mL) warm water

Directions:

Mix the ingredients in a large bowl. Knead for ten to fifteen minutes until clay is moldable. (Have students help with this part!)

Use the above clay by rolling out to 1/2" thickness and allowing students to cut out shapes with cookie cutters. Students can also design their own shapes and cut out with a butter knife or make a free-form creation with this clay. Preheat oven to 325°F (180° C). Place clay creations on baking sheets and bake for one hour, or until all moisture is gone. Cool completely. Students can now paint their creations. Spray with clear shellac, if desired.

Note: Recipe can be cut in half. Food coloring may be added when the clay is being mixed.

Cornstarch Clay

Ingredients:

4 cups (1L) flour

2 3/4 cup (625 mL) cornstarch

2 3/4 cup (625 mL) salt

2 3/4 cup (625 mL) water

Directions:

Combine the flour, cornstarch and salt in a large bowl. Add 2 cups of the water and knead thoroughly. Add remaining water, 1/2 cup at a time, until dough is no longer sticky. (You may not need all of the water.)

Give each child a portion of the clay. Have them make letter or number shapes, or a free-form creation. Allow to air-dry thoroughly. Students can then paint their work. Note: Food coloring or tempera-paint powder can be added while combining the first three ingredients.

❧ Colorful Creations ❧

Materials: Plastic bags; food coloring; rice, sand, salt, or cornmeal

Directions:

Place rice, sand, salt, or cornmeal in plastic bag. Add a few drops of desired food coloring. Close bag tightly and shake well. Use colored medium for making three-dimensional pictures, or to trace writing, spelling, or language development words.

Recipes

Barley-Corn Soup

(The Country Mouse's Favorite Soup!)

Ingredients:

16 cups (4L) beef broth

1 cup (250 mL) barley

1 1/2 teaspoons (8 mL) sage

1/2 teaspoon (2 mL) salt

1/4 teaspoon (1 mL) garlic powder

2 cups (500 mL) canned corn, drained

2 cups (500 mL) sliced canned mushrooms, drained

Directions:

In a large pot, or slow cooker, combine broth, barley, sage, salt, and garlic powder. Bring to a boil; reduce heat. Cover and simmer for one hour. Add drained corn and mushrooms. Cover and simmer an additional 20 to 30 minutes. Enjoy!

Crunchy Carrot Cookies

(The Town Mouse's Favorite Healthy Snack!)

Ingredients:

1/2 cup (125mL) margarine or butter

1 cup (250 mL) brown sugar

1 cup (250 mL) shredded carrots

1/2 cup (125 mL) orange juice

1 egg

1 1/2 cup (375 mL) flour

1/2 teaspoon (2 mL) baking soda

1/2 teaspoon (2mL) salt

1 cup (250 mL) quick-cooking oats

3/4 cup (175 mL) sunflower seeds

Directions:

1. Heat oven to 350º F (190º C). Lightly grease cookie sheet.

2. In a large bowl, combine margarine, sugar, carrots, juice, and egg; mix well.

3. Add flour, soda, and salt; mix well.

4. Stir in the oats and sunflower seeds; blend.

5. Spoon by rounded teaspoonfuls onto cookie sheet. (Leave a little bit of room, they will spread). Bake for 10 to 12 minutes. Remove and cool 1 minute. Remove from cookie sheet and cool completely.

Makes approximately 35 cookies.

Wheat Cakes

This culminating activity is designed to allow students to enjoy the same experience the little red hen had eating her delicious wheat cake.

Have the students help in making and mixing the wheat cake batter. Provide an activity, such as the puzzle on page 40, for them to do while they are waiting their turn.

The following recipe is designed for cupcakes so that each student has their own cake. While cupcakes are baking, reread *The Little Red Hen* or write and illustrate a class language experience story about the baking project.

Ingredients:

1 cup (250 mL) margarine or butter

1 cup (250 mL) or 1/2 cup (125mL) honey

2 eggs

1 1/4 cup (300 mL) milk or buttermilk

1 teaspoon (5 mL) vanilla

2 cups (500 mL) wheat flour

1 cup (250 mL) quick-cooking rolled oats

1 1/2 teaspoons (7 mL) baking soda

1/2 teaspoon (2 mL) salt

Optional:

1/2 cup (125 mL) nuts; 1 cup (250 mL) chocolate chips; 1 medium banana, mashed

Directions:

1. Heat oven to 350° F (190° C). Line cupcake tins with paper cupcake liners.

2. In large bowl, mix margarine, sugar, and eggs; beat well.

3. Add the milk and vanilla; blend.

4. Stir in flour, oats, soda, and salt; mix well.

5. Add optional items, if desired.

6. Spoon batter into the cupcake liners. Bake for 20 minutes, then test center to see if done. Remove and let cool slightly. Remove from tins; let cool completely or enjoy while still warm.

   Makes 24 wheat cupcakes.

62

Sensation Stations!

Here is a fun culminating activity that will allow your students to have a closure experience to the reading of *The Town Mouse and the Country Mouse*! The activity is actually a cycle of five rotating stations. There is a station for each sense—SEE, HEAR, SMELL, TASTE, and FEEL.

Just follow the directions outlined on the following pages and your entire class will be guaranteed to have a super-sensational time!

Preparation

Gather and prepare necessary materials as outlined for each station. Enlist the help of parent volunteers to be a leader at each station.

Divide the Class into Five Teams:

Try to make sure that the teams are balanced in capabilities and behavior.

Rotate through the Five Stations:

Seat student teams at the center where they will begin. Each station takes approximately 10 minutes to complete. Therefore, at the end of each 10 minute period, ring a bell, or blow a whistle, to signify that it is time to rotate to the next station. It will take approximately 1 hour, including a little extra time for rotating, for all teams to experience all stations.

Sensation Stations *(cont.)*

Station One: SEE

Think Twice Mice Pictures

Preparation:

1. Reproduce the mouse head on page 70 ten times. Color, cut out, and mount each one on the front of a file folder. Cut out the eye and ear areas through the first layer of all ten folders.

2. Inside each folder glue a colorful picture (calendar pictures work well) so that parts of it show through the mouse head openings.

3. Place prepared folders, drawing paper, pencils, and crayons at Station One.

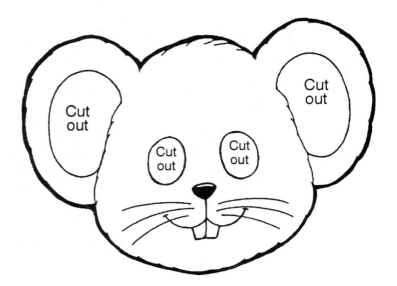

Activity:

The leader gives each student one of the folders, cautioning them not to open it. Think once, think twice! What picture is behind the mouse's head? Have children draw what they think they will see when they open the folder. When done illustrating, they ask the leader for permission to peek. Watch the surprised looks when they see what their picture really is! If enough time, allow each student to illustrate a second folder's hidden picture.

Sensation Stations

Station Two: HEAR

Mouse Messages

Preparation: Write the following messages on 5" x 7" cards (or on cards in the shape of a mouse's silhouette).

Town and Country Mouse went for a walk.

Town Mouse smelled a pretty flower.

Country Mouse cooked a special dinner.

"Do you want to come to town with me?"

Country Mouse liked the bright lights.

"Look at the goodies to eat on the table!"

"I like the country life the best!"

"Barley-corn soup is the yummiest!"

Activity:

Have the team sit close together so that they can whisper into each other's ears. The leader shuffles the cards and places them face down on the table. A student picks up the top card and passes it to the leader. The leader whispers what it says into the first team member's ear. The team members must listen carefully because the mouse message can not be repeated. The team member then turns and whispers to the next person what they think was whispered into their ear. The message continues around until it reaches the last team member. This team member then tells aloud what the mouse message was. What a surprise to hear how the message changed!

Station Three: SMELL

Can You Tell the Smell?

Materials: Hammer; nails; ten baby food jars with lids; contact paper; ten cotton balls; ten "smelly" items (e.g., peppermint, orange, and cinnamon extracts, peanut butter, cocoa, coffee, pickle juice, garlic clove, onion, pineapple); pictures of smelly items mounted onto 3" x 3" cardboard squares (page 66)

Preparation: Cover the outside of the glass jars with contact paper. Punch a hole in lid with hammer and nail. Place a cotton ball in each jar. Add a "smell" to each jar. Screw lids onto jars. Label contents on tape attached to bottom.

Activity:

The leader asks team if they think they can figure out what is in each jar by using just their sense of smell. Show the team the ten pictures. Ask them to smell to see which picture matches which jar. When they think they have a match, they place the appropriate card on top of the jar. When all cards have been placed, the leader checks the answer by showing the bottom of the jar. Let the team try again after mixing jars and pictures.

Picture Cards for Sensation Station 3

*See suggested activity, page 65

peppermint

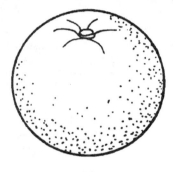

orange

cinnamon

peanuts

chocolate

coffee

pickle

garlic

onion

pineapple

Sensation Stations *(cont.)*

Station Four: TASTE

Mouse Treats

Ingredients: Canned pear halves, (well-drained); mini-chocolate chips; miniature marshmallows (colored ones are fun); licorice laces; cheese slices (optional)

Materials: small paper plates; plastic forks

Activity:

Have each child place a cheese slice on a paper plate. Put a pear half on top of it. Position chocolate chip eyes and nose at the narrow end. Using thumb and forefinger, flatten two miniature marshmallows to become ears. Add licorice tail and whiskers. Admire and enjoy!

Station Five: FEEL

Sock It to Me!

Materials: 10 large socks; 10 plastic containers that can fit into the "foot" of the sock (e.g., yogurt or margarine containers); 10 items (suggestions: key, little play car, necklace, feather, comb, rubber bands, sea shells, spoon, eraser, barrette, coins); pictures of chosen items mounted onto 3" x 3" pieces of cardboard.

Preparation: Push a plastic container into the bottom of each sock. Add an item to each one.

Activity:

The leader tells the team that they are going to have to match the pictures to the items in each sock, but they can't look at them. They have to put their hands into the sock and feel the items. Hand out pictures to the team members and allow them to work together to match the pictures to the correct sock. When they have placed a picture on top of all the socks, the leader checks to see if they are correct.

Bulletin Board

Objectives

This interactive bulletin board has been designed to introduce and review the five senses. It can also be adapted to use to reinforce math, reading, and language skills.

Materials

Butcher paper; colored construction paper; envelope; scissors; glue; stapler or pins; crayons or markers

Construction

1. Reproduce the mouse body parts and cheese five times onto appropriately colored paper. Cut out. Add details. Glue bodies together following helpful plan on page 69.

2. Label each cheese with a sense word: SEE, HEAR, SMELL, TASTE, FEEL.

3. Cover the background with butcher paper. Staple mice onto bulletin board. Staple envelope in lower corner. Place cheese wedges in envelope. Add title.

Directions

As an introduction to the senses unit, gather students around bulletin board display. Have them identify what the first mouse is pointing to—his eye. Explain that our bodies have senses. Senses are "knowing what is around us by using our body parts." When we see, our eyes are using the sense called "SEE" (seeing). Remove the cheese wedge labeled SEE and place it under the appropriate mouse. Continue with the remaining four senses. If students already have an initial awareness of the five senses, allow them to be more interactive and choose a wedge first and decide which mouse is displaying that sense. To use the bulletin board as a review, allow students to label each sense during their free time.

To use the bulletin board in an interactive way, place information/answers onto the mice bodies and the question/facts onto the cheese wedges (you may need to make additional cheese wedges). Place the wedges in the envelope; allow the students to practice during free or center time. For example, to review addition problems to 10, label each mouse with a sum (3,5,7,8, 10). On cheese wedges, write problems (2+5, 4+4, 5+5, 1+2...). Write the correct sum on back of the cheese wedges. Students match cheese wedges to correct mouse. When all the wedges have been used, students turn over the wedges to self-correct.

Bulletin Board *(cont.)*

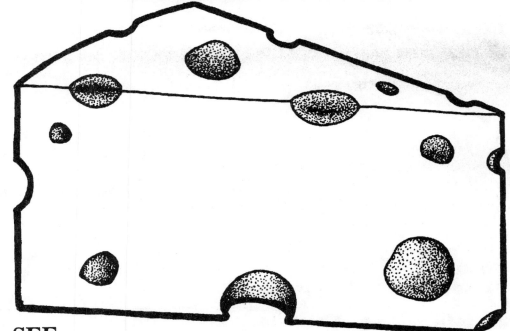

Cheese
Pattern

Make 5

SEE

HEAR

Positioning
the Arms

SMELL

TASTE

FEEL

Bulletin Board *(cont.)*

Bulletin Board (cont.)

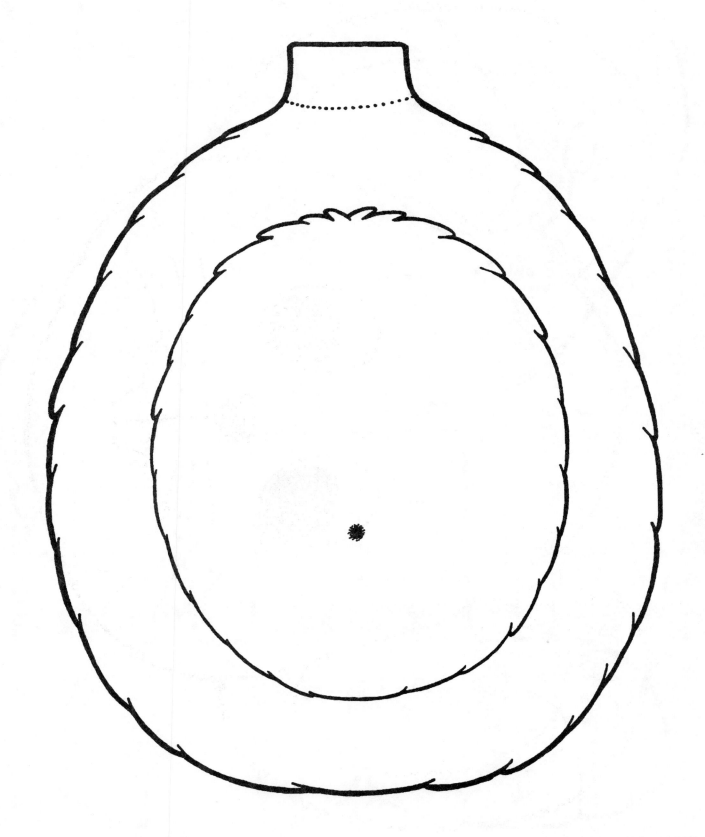

Bulletin Board *(cont.)*

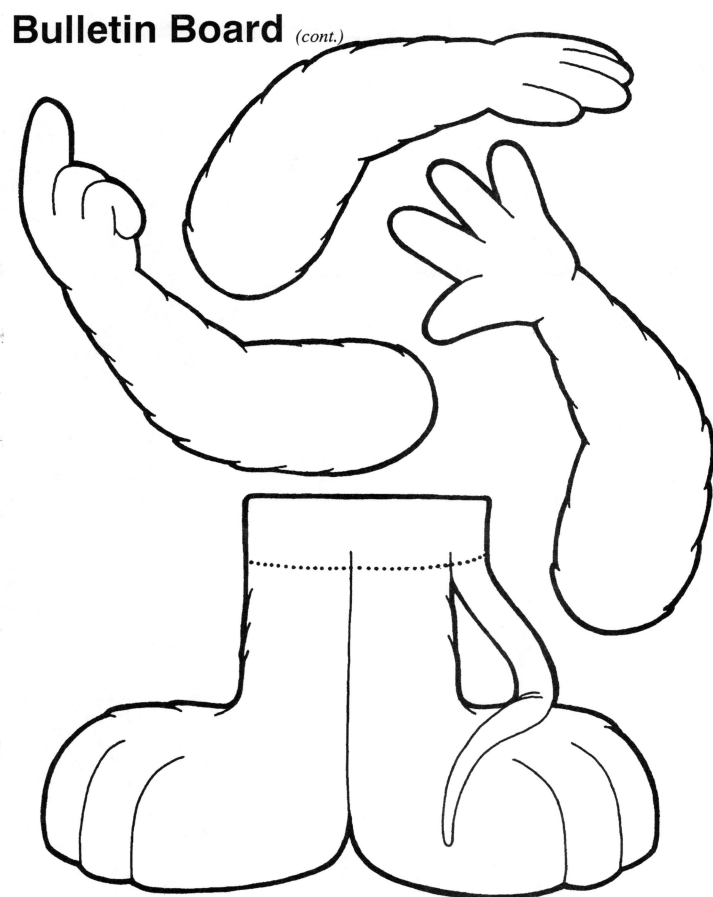

Creating Learning Centers

A Learning Center is a special area set aside in the classroom for the study of a specific topic. Typically, a Learning Center contains a variety of activities and materials that teach, reinforce, and enrich skills and concepts. Because students learn in different ways and at different rates, a Learning Center can be a valuable means of providing for these differences. Activities in a given center should be based on the abilities, needs, and interests of the students in your classroom. Learning Centers are equally appropriate for cooperative group and individual use.

How to Create Your Senses Learning Centers

- Choose five areas within the classroom which can be designated as a specific sense center. These areas may be tables, mats, desks, or floor space.
- Determine the skills/concepts activities to be taught/reinforced at each sense center area (e.g., SMELL–have different flowering plants on a table with paper noses cut so that students can draw the flowers on the noses as they smell them).
- Prepare extensions using the ideas suggested throughout the senses thematic unit.
- Gather all materials needed, plus any needed parent helpers for supervising, and set up center areas.

Scheduling Center Time

- Plan a schedule where groups of children are rotated to different activities. For example, one group can be attending a teacher-directed lesson, while the second group completes seat work, and the third group is at the Learning Center.
- Assign individuals or small groups to the center, according to diagnosed needs.
- Have a set Center Time. Assign a different group each day to work at the center during that time.

Record Keeping

- Use a simple Record Form (see Page 74) to record all students' names and check them off as they complete a particular project.
- Make a monthly calendar for each student; store in a three-ring binder at the center. Record information on the appropriate spaces.
- Keep a file box with students' names listed alphabetically on index cards. Record notes and activities completed on the cards.

Record Form

Name																
1.																
2.																
3.																
4.																
5.																
6.																
7.																
8.																
9.																
10.																
11.																
12.																
13.																
14.																
15.																
16.																
17.																
18.																
19.																
20.																
21.																
22.																
23.																
24.																
25.																
26.																
27.																
28.																
29.																
30.																

Request for Help

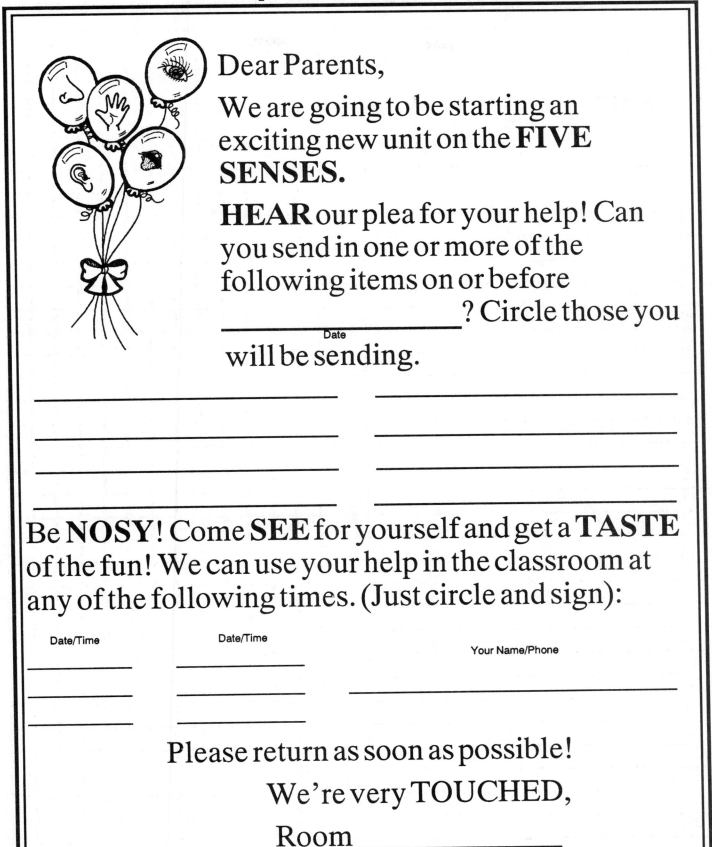

Dear Parents,

We are going to be starting an exciting new unit on the **FIVE SENSES.**

HEAR our plea for your help! Can you send in one or more of the following items on or before _____? Circle those you will be sending.

Date

_____   _____

_____   _____

_____   _____

Be **NOSY**! Come **SEE** for yourself and get a **TASTE** of the fun! We can use your help in the classroom at any of the following times. (Just circle and sign):

Date/Time   Date/Time   Your Name/Phone

_____ _____   _____

_____ _____

Please return as soon as possible!

We're very TOUCHED,

Room _____

Award/Thank You

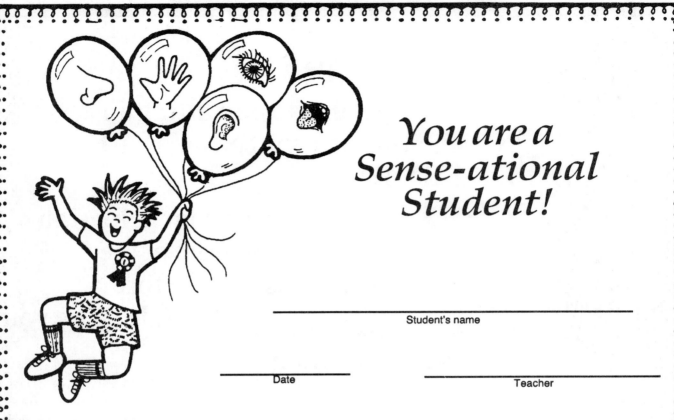

You are a Sense-ational Student!

_____
Student's name

_____   _____
Date   Teacher

Thank You!

It's so nice you said, "I will help!"

_____
Teacher

Dear

 # 270 Thematic Unit — Five Senses

Clip Art

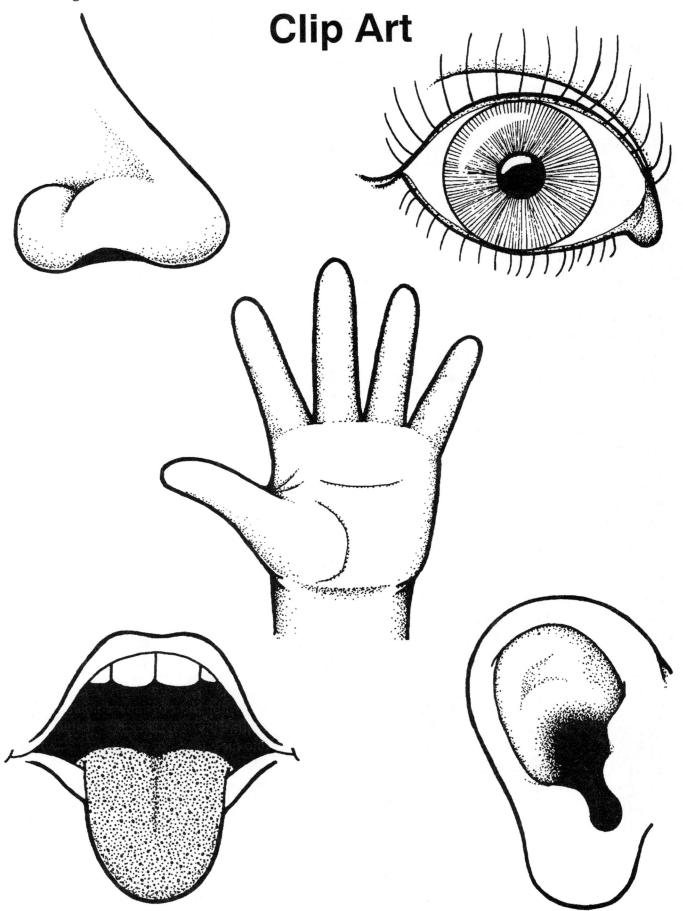

Bibliography

Aliki. *My Five Senses.* Crowell, 1962.
Alington, R. & Kathleen Krull. *Tasting.* Raintree, 1980.
Berry, Ray. *Teach Me About Tasting.* Grolier, 1986.
Dubov, Christine. *Where Is Your Nose?* St. Martin, 1986.
Friday, Beverly. *Eyes, Ears, Nose, and Mouth.* Standard, 1986
Galdone, Paul. *Jack and the Beanstalk.* Ticknor and Fields, 1982. (or other version)
Moncure, Jane. *The Touch Book.* Children's Press, 1982.
Parramon, J. M. et. al. *Five Senses (5 book set).* Barron, 1985.
Sattler, Helen. *Noses Are Special.* Abingdon, 1982.

Mice

Cauley, Lorinda Bryan. *The Town Mouse and the Country Mouse.* Penguin, 1994.
Horner, Susan. *Mice.* Grolier Limited, 1985.
Kraus, Robert. *Where Are You Going, Little Mouse?* Mulberry Books, 1986.
Lionni, Leo. *Frederick.* Pantheon Press, 1967.
Numeroff Laura. *If You Give a Mouse a Cookie.* Scholastic Inc., 1985

Chickens

Back, C. and J. Olesen. *Chicken and Egg.* Silver Burdett, 1986.
Galdone, Paul. *The Little Red Hen.* Houghton Mifflin, 1973.
Hutchins, Pat. *Rosie's Walk.* Macmillan, 1971.
Johnson, Sylvia. *Inside an Egg.* Lerner Publishing, 1982.
Kellogg, Steven. *Chicken Little.* Mulberry Books, 1985.
Wonder Starters. *Eggs.* Wonder Books, 1974.

Wheat/Bread

Hoban, Russell. *Bread and Jam for Frances.* Harper & Row, 1970.
Wonder Starters. *Bread.* Wonder Books, 1974.

Teacher Created Materials

TCM 300   Literature Activities for Young Children *(Brown Bear, Brown Bear, What Do You See?)*
TCM 301   Literature Activities for Young Children *(The Carrot Seed; Green Eggs and Ham)*
TCM 306   Literature Activities for Young Children (variety)
TCM 213   The Senses
TCM 212   Food and Nutrition
TCM 151   September Monthly Activities (Apples Whole Language Unit)
TCM 090   ABC Crafts and Cooking
TCM 071   Grocery Bag Art—Farm

Answer Key

Page 11

Up   Loud
Down   Soft
Up   Soft
Down   Loud

If answers vary, have students explain their reasoning.

Page 31

 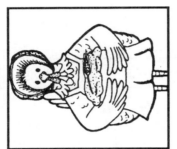

 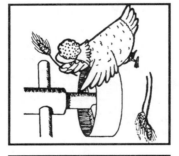

 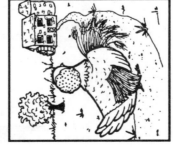

Page 40

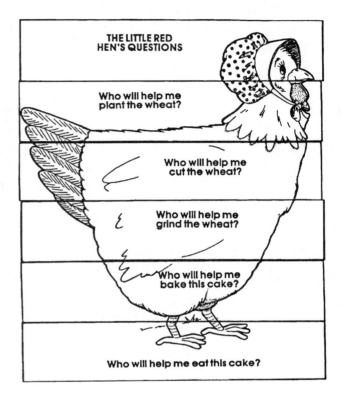

Page 47

MB   R
R   MB

Page 52

Answers will vary.